SCUBA SCHOOLS
INTERNATIONAL

Deep Diving

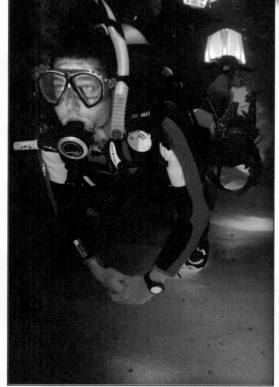

DISCLAIMER:

The information contained in the SSI training materials is intended to give an individual enrolled in a training course a broad perspective of the diving activity. There are many recommendations and suggestions regarding the use of standard and specialized equipment for the activity. Not all of the equipment discussed in the training material can, or will, be used in this activity. The choice of equipment and techniques used in the course is determined by the location of the activity, the environmental conditions and other factors.

A choice of equipment and techniques cannot be made until the dive site is surveyed immediately prior to the dive. Based on the dive site, the decision should be made regarding which equipment and techniques shall be used. The decision belongs to the dive leader and the individual enrolled in the training course.

The intent of all SSI training materials is to give individuals as much information as possible in order for individuals to make their own decisions regarding the diving activity, what equipment should be used and what specific techniques may be needed. The ultimate decision on when and how to dive is for the individual diver to make.

First Edition
  First Printing, 12/91
  Second Printing, 2/93

Second Edition
  First Printing, 6/96
  Second Printing, 3/98
  Third Printing, 7/00

Third Edition
  First Printing, 1/04
  Second Printing, 10/05

Fourth Edition
  First Printing, 2/09

PRINTED IN THE USA

SCUBA SCHOOLS
INTERNATIONAL

2619 Canton Court • Fort Collins, CO 80525-4498
(970) 482-0883 • Fax (970) 482-6157

Contents

Section 5: Your Repetitive Deep Diving

Appendix

Acknowledgements

Editor in Chief	Doug McNeese
Writers	Laurie Humpal Hal Watts
Manager of Development	Suzanne Fletcher
Graphic Designers	Lori Evans, David Pratt Jennifer Silos
Cover Photo	James E. Bruning,
Photographers	James E. Bruning, Randy Pfizenmaier
Contributing Photographers	Black Durgeon, Paolo Lilla, Rick Murchison
Technical Editors	Walt Amidon, Dan Barrows, Daryl Bauer, James Bruning, Robert Kennedy, Doug McNeese, Kirk Mortensen, Linda Nelson, Eric Peterson, Jeff Powelson, Warren Roseberry, Ed Salamone, Craig Simons, Sid Stovall, Ron Tinker, Craig Willemsen, Marjorie Young

Special thanks to the staff at Ocean Sports, Randy Pfizenmaier and Ikelite for going the extra mile in the production of this manual.

Preface

You will see that each section includes several unique icons to highlight information or add information that relates to the text near it. In some cases, these icons point out information directly associated with the section objectives, while in other cases, the icon indicates a continuing education opportunity. While these icons are designed to help you learn and retain information, they also provide you with an easy reference to important information as you study.

Pearl

"Pearl" the oyster (originally named "Hey!"), is found throughout the text to point out information that we believe is key to a new diver's success. The "pearls of wisdom" that our oyster friend highlights are designed to help you meet section objectives, assist in answering study guide questions and may be used in group discussions with your instructor.

Continuing Education

At Scuba Schools International, we believe that one of the keys to achieving and maintaining success as a diver is taking the "next step" via continuing education. To reinforce that belief, we have put a Continuing Education icon next to topics that correspond to continuing education opportunities available to you through your SSI Dealer. Your SSI Instructor or Dealer will be happy to answer any questions you may have about the continuing education courses listed throughout this manual.

Environment

SSI has always supported and promoted environmental awareness and believes that care for the environment should be a standard part of diver education from start to finish. For these reasons, an environmental icon has been included to highlight important environmental issues as they relate to divers and the underwater world. Topics that you will find the environmental icon next to include the importance of buoyancy control, reef appreciation and conservation, and using your equipment in an environmentally friendly way.

International Use

To meet international English language recommendations, some of the words you come across in this manual may look misspelled. The following is a list of these words in American English and their International counterparts.

American English	International Counterpart
Center	Centre
Meter	Metre
Gray	Grey
Aluminum	Aluminium

Throughout the manual, imperial measurements are listed first followed by the metric conversion. The following conversion units were used to convert the various measurements:

1 ATA (Atmospheres Absolute) = 14.7 psi (pounds per square inch)

1 ATA = 33 fsw (feet of sea water)

1 ATA = 10.33 metres of sea water

1 ATA = 1 bar

1 Metre = 3.28 feet

$C° = (F° - 32) ÷ 1.8$

1 kg (kilogram) = 2.2 lbs (pounds)

1 km (kilometre) = .621 miles

Note: For greater ease, many of the conversions in this text have been rounded to the nearest whole number, and may not reflect the exact conversion.

Be Ready for Your Journey

SSI
SCUBA SCHOOLS
INTERNATIONAL

Intro

Welcome

Many of the more exciting, intriguing dive sites are found in deeper water. This manual covers the knowledge, skills and equipment necessary for the Deep Diving specialty.

Without proper training this kind of diving can put you at risk. To plan your dives properly you must first know how to prevent any of the potential risks involved in deep diving. This course will provide you with the information to make deep dives comfortably and confidently.

Our goal is to prepare you for your Deep Diving adventure and make sure you have a good experience.

Be Ready for Your Journey

All of our specialty courses are based on our signature training method — the SSI Diver Diamond. To become a comfortable and confident diver, it takes 4 ingredients:

Proper Knowledge

As in all of SSI training programs, knowledge is power and replaces fears and fantasies with correct information. In this program, you will acquire the specific knowledge related to the Deep Diving Specialty.

Proper Skills

Repetition is the mother of all skills. Under the guidance of your SSI Dive Professional, you will learn the specific skills and techniques needed to make dives below 60 feet/18 metres.

Proper Equipment

The safest way to dive is in your own personally fitted Total Diving System. For this and all SSI Continuing Education courses, you may need additional equipment to perform these dives.

Proper Experience

Gaining the knowledge, skills and equipment to make these deeper dives is only one part of the journey. Going diving is the only way you can gain the actual experience needed to become a Deep Diver.

How Far Do You Want to Go?

If you believe the journey is just as important as the destination, then SSI's Continuing Education is for you. Taking specialties is a great way to hone your skills and learn some new ones. Continuing Education is exciting and limitless. It is your chance to begin exploring beyond the surface. Choose your personal combination of training and diving experience to reach your diving goals today!

SSI's Continuing Education courses are all menu-based home study programs. These specialty courses are designed so that you can learn at your own pace when it's convenient for you. Menu-based means you can take courses in a combined manner or one at a time based on your personal interest. Simply choose from specialties like, Photography, Enriched Air Nitrox, Wreck, Navigation, Night and Limited Visibility and you're on your way.

Getting involved is easy! If you're not sure which specialties you want to try, sign up for the Advanced Adventurer program. You will be able to take 5 dives and try 5 different specialties. Upon completion you will be recognized with an Advanced Adventurer card. These dives also count towards your rating if you choose to continue your training in one of the specialty areas covered.

For detailed information regarding SSI Specialty programs visit www.diveSSI.com

5 OR MORE LOGGED DIVES

LEVEL OF EXPERIENCE: 1

Complete the SSI Open Water Diver course & get this card!

12 OR MORE LOGGED DIVES

LEVEL OF EXPERIENCE: 2

Complete Level 2 dives & 2 Specialty Courses.

24 OR MORE LOGGED DIVES

LEVEL OF EXPERIENCE: 3

Complete Level 3 dives & 4 Specialty Courses.

50 OR MORE LOGGED DIVES

LEVEL OF EXPERIENCE: 4

Complete Level 4 dives, 4 Specialty Courses & the Diver Stress & Rescue Course.

AVAILABLE SPECIALTIES — *Take one or take them all!*

- ◆ Adaptive Scuba Diving
- ◆ Boat Diving
- ◆ Computer Diving
- ◆ Deep Diving
- ◆ Digital Underwater Photography
- ◆ Diver Stress & Rescue
- ◆ Dry Suit Diving
- ◆ Emergency Training
  - – First Aid & CPR
  - – Emergency Oxygen
  - – AED
  - – Bloodborne Pathogens
- ◆ Enriched Air Nitrox

- ◆ Equipment Techniques
- ◆ Navigation
- ◆ Night and Limited Visibility Diving
- ◆ Perfect Buoyancy
- ◆ Search & Recovery
- ◆ Waves, Tides & Currents
- ◆ Wreck Diving
- ◆ Technical Extended Range
  - – Advanced Nitrox
  - – Technical Foundations
  - – Decompression Procedures
  - – Advanced Decompression
  - – Normoxic Trimix

You can become a Dive Leader once you have completed Level 4!
Ask your SSI Dive Center for complete details.

Instructor Levels

Quality Divers Start with Qualified Instructors

Other Instructor Programs

◆ Specialty Instructor
◆ Diver Stress & Rescue Instructor
◆ Enriched Air Nitrox Instructor
◆ Scuba Rangers Instructor
◆ Technical Extended Range
  – Advanced Nitrox Instructor
  – Technical Foundations Instructor
  – Decompression Procedures Instructor
  – Advanced Decompression Procedures Instructor
  – Normoxic Trimix Instructor
  – TechXR Instructor Trainer

REWARDS FOR EXPERIENCE

No Training Required!

Taking a specific number of specialties and continuing your pursuit of dives allows you to earn higher levels of diver ratings. SSI Ratings are the only ratings in the industry that combine training and experience requirements, proving that SSI Ratings are truly earned.

Reward yourself as you reach new milestones in your diving adventures!

About SSI

Scuba Schools International grew out of the passion of a few avid divers who were intent on making it possible for anyone to learn to scuba dive.

SSI provides education materials, dive training and scuba certification for divers, dive instructors, dive centers and dive resorts around the world. Since 1970, SSI has expanded to 27 International Offices, doing business in 110 countries with training materials in 25 languages representing over 2,400 dive centers

and resorts. SSI Certification Cards are welcomed all over the planet, wherever you choose to dive.

Scuba Schools International is clearly a name you can trust in the diving community and we attribute that success to uncompromising standards and a focus on quality not quantity.

Involvement

As well as being an industry leader, SSI is also a founding member of the industry's standards body in the USA and abroad — in the USA, it's the RSTC (Recreational Scuba Training Council) and in Europe, it's the WRSTC and the EU (European Standards — EN 14153-1-3 for divers and 144413-1-2 for scuba instructors).

Reward Yourself. You Deserve it.

Becoming a certified Deep Diver is an achievement. Be sure to reward yourself for reaching this major milestone with an SSI Deep Diving certification card. This is an opportunity to commemorate your hard-earned accomplishment.

Where to Go From Here.

We are certain that your journey through Deep Diving will be everything you imagined and more. Don't forget you can always combine other specialties to increase your diving knowledge — the possibilities are limitless. Now, let's go have some fun!

Your Total Diving System & Deep Diving

When you get involved in deep diving, you should be more selective in the equipment that you use. Proper selection, adjustment, use and care of equipment is extremely important for this specialized type of diving.

Section 1 Objectives

After completing this section you will

◆ Understand how to prepare your Total Diving System for Deep Diving,

◆ Be able to list any special equipment that is needed for Deep Diving,

◆ Know what surface equipment is needed for Deep Diving,

Scuba Equipment — The Total Diving System

In your SSI Open Water Diver course, you learned that scuba diving is an equipment intensive sport. In fact, without a properly fitted, well-maintained Total Diving System, humans could not stay for prolonged periods under water. It allows us to see, breathe, and float, as well as protect us from the environment. As we venture deeper, our scuba equipment becomes even more valuable to our comfort and safety. The greater distance between you and the surface increases the need for you to be highly skilled and able to rely on your own equipment, in case of an emergency.

As divers venture deeper, their scuba equipment becomes more valuable to their comfort and safety.

Using a high-quality Total Diving System decreases the chance of a problem occurring. In fact, today's high-quality equipment, when properly maintained, will provide you with years of comfortable diving.

If you are interested in learning more about equipment and how to maintain it, your local SSI Dive Center offers a specialty course on Equipment Techniques. Also, your Instructor can offer an equipment consultation for you.

Let us take a look at the basic pieces of equipment used on every dive, and how the demands on the equipment differ for deep diving.

Air Delivery System

The first piece of equipment we will look at is the Air Delivery System, because it is the most sensitive and most important piece of equipment for the diver. For shallow diving, just about any Air Delivery System is adequate. However for deep diving, you should not settle for an "adequate" Air Delivery System. Deep diving requires a top-quality, high-performance Air Delivery System that will perform well at any depth. Let us quickly look at the reasons why.

Deep diving requires a top-quality, high-performance Air Delivery System that will perform well at any depth.

First- & Second-Stage Regulators

Just as your air consumption increases with depth and pressure, so will breathing resistance. As the diver descends, water pressure continues to increase on the body. This pressure would make it extremely difficult, if not impossible to inhale without the aid of the much greater pressure in the intermediate stage of your first-stage regulator. When you inhale, the pressure in the intermediate stage of your first-stage regulator allows you to inhale against the pressure as though no external pressure existed. There are other factors that can contribute to breathing resistance such as low cylinder pressure (below 500 PSI or 35 bars), rapid breathing and poor Air Delivery System maintenance. Since your cylinder pressure and breathing rate can be easily monitored, let us take a look at first- and second-stage regulators — and how they perform.

Breathe Easy

A high-quality balanced regulator breathes almost easier at depth than it does at the surface.

DIVER DIAMOND
SSI

Today's first- and second-stage regulators can be purchased in one of two designs: balanced or unbalanced. For deep diving, it is recommended that your first- and second-stage regulators be "balanced." Balanced first-and second-stage regulators are designed to maintain excellent breathing performance all the way down to very low cylinder pressure, while unbalanced units will become harder breathing at greater depths and at cylinder pressures below 600 or 700 psi (41 or 48 bars).

Your Air Delivery System should deliver all the air that two divers may need in an air-sharing situation.

So, in summary, deep diving requires first- and second-stage regulators that are balanced, will give you plenty of volume at increased depth and a second-stage regulator that is easy to exhale through. The physical demands on the diver and the equipment increases with depth. Inexpensive first- and second-stage regulators may not deliver an adequate amount of air at depth, especially when a diver becomes stressed and begins to breathe more rapidly. Your Air Delivery System should deliver all the air that two divers may need in an air-sharing situation, so both divers can breathe at the same time with separate mouthpieces.

A primary second-stage paired with a secondary second-stage is a common configuration for an alternate air source.

Alternate Air Source

It is tempting for many divers to buy an alternate air source of lesser quality since it is only a "back up" second-stage regulator. However, should you experience problems with your primary second-stage, or should you need to share air at a great depth, the last thing you will want is a poor quality alternate air source. Most manufacturers offer a high quality alternate air source that will compliment your primary second-stage nicely.

The air integrated inflator source combines the alternate air source with the power inflator.

Several manufacturers have a unit that combines the alternate air source into the power inflator to create an air integrated inflator source. This system eliminates one hose and makes it easy to find the extra mouthpiece in a stressful situation. No matter which system you choose, the most important aspect is that your first-stage must be of high enough quality and performance to allow two divers to share air from the same system at depth.

Some divers choose an independent air source, either in addition to one of the above systems or to stand alone as an alternate air source. The difference with this system is that it contains its own cylinder and regulator system that operate independently. Again, this system should be of high enough quality to breathe easily at depth and hold enough air to make a normal ascent to the surface from a depth of 100-130 feet (30-39 metres). Consult your SSI Dive Center for more information about purchasing an independent air source.

An independent air source contains its own cylinder and first- and second-stage regulator system that operate independently.

It is recommended that any independent air source has a cylinder with at least 12 cubic feet of air.

Cylinder

When selecting a cylinder for deep diving, choose one that supplies enough air to complete the dive comfortably (usually double cylinders).

As you become more comfortable with deep diving, your air consumption rate should drop and allow you to complete your dive with a 71.2 or 80 cubic foot cylinder (1981-2264 litres). However, if your air consumption rate is high, it may be acceptable to use double cylinders, a single 95 cubic foot (2688 litres), or a larger cylinder, if necessary.

Buoyancy Control System

The next piece of equipment that is important for deep diving is the buoyancy control system or BC. Be sure that the one you select provides enough lift to bring another diver to the surface from depth.

It is recommended that a BC should have enough lift to bring yourself and another diver to the surface from depth.

Remember, diving is equipment-intensive and a buddy sport. Each diver should wear equipment that will help a buddy in an emergency.

The deeper you dive, the more critical your equipment is. It is recommended that a buoyancy control system should have adequate lift (25-55 lbs. at sea level), and be equipped with a working power inflator.

Diving Instruments

Your diving instruments become much more critical to your safety when deep diving because depth, time, direction and air must be constantly monitored. The best dive plan is only as good as the follow-through. The follow-through includes making sure you stay at or shallower than your planned depth, stay down no longer than your planned time, and save enough air for your ascent and safety stop and still have a 500 PSI (35 bar) safety margin.

◆ **Diving Computer.** Although the diving computer is an option for deep divers, it is highly recommended; those who use them on a regular basis consider them mandatory. These units are used to monitor your no-decompression limits, or to advise you what depth to stop at if you inadvertently get into a decompression situation. Most computers give you depth, bottom time, an ascent alarm if you are exceeding the proper ascent rate, remaining no-decompression time, a memory for dive log information, your surface interval between dives, scrolling for no-decompression limits for the next dive and, in some models, the water temperature and cylinder pressure.

Some computer manufacturers have recommendations for computer failure, as does the AAUS, American Academy of Underwater Sciences. In the event of computer failure, most recommend that divers surface using normal ascent procedures, and stay out of the water for at least 24 hours.

It is not safe to switch to the dive tables without backup instruments and an up-to-date DiveLog.

The benefit of a diving computer is that it increases your bottom time by giving you credit for all the time that you spend at shallower depths. This is handy when multi-level diving. As with all specialized pieces of equipment, you should receive additional training in how to use a computer before diving with one. You will also need to learn about how your particular model of computer operates because they all offer different features. If you are interested in learning more about computers, ask your local SSI store about a Computer Diving Specialty course.

The benefit of a diving computer is that it increases your bottom time by giving you credit for all the time that you spent at shallower depths.

Each diver must be equipped with his or her own computer. Computers should not be shared while diving. Your SSI Dive Center can help you and your buddy select the best dive computer to fit your needs.

While you may not encounter analog instruments in your diving career, it is a good idea to know how to use them if you do. The most accurate analog gauges at depth are the oil-filled, the gas-filled and the bourdon tube. However, no analog gauge will be completely accurate at depth.

Digital gauges are also available that display your depth, pressure and other information digitally. These consoles may, or may not, include a dive computer. Equipment manufacturers claim that digital gauges are more accurate than analog gauges and the only maintenance they require is new batteries.

No matter which style you use, make sure the gauge has a maximum depth indicator so you have a record of the deepest point you reached during your dive. This number must be used when figuring any repetitive dive plans.

Digital gauges are more accurate than analog gauges and the only maintenance they require is new batteries.

◆ **Submersible Pressure Gauges.** The SPG is also an important part of the instrument console. As with depth gauges, the SPG can be either analog or digital. The pressure gauge needs to be as accurate as possible, so you should check it periodically by comparing it to another gauge. You can do this by hooking up one gauge after the other to the same cylinder.

◆ **Compass.** A compass is valuable in deep diving because you must be able to navigate accurately back to the point where you will begin your ascent to the 15 foot (5 metre) safety stop. This is particularly important when boat diving, or when diving in limited visibility. As with all your other instruments, your compass should be of high quality. To learn more about compasses, ask your local SSI Dive Center about a specialty course on Navigation.

◆ **Timing Device.** Because bottom time is not flexible when deep diving, an accurate timing device must be used. One type of timing device is the dive watch. It should have a unidirectional bezel that can be set to indicate the start of the dive. Digital watches are also popular. These dive timers can be attached to your console, or may be part of your digital instruments or computer. The advantage of a digital bottom timer when deep diving is that you do not have to remember to set it or turn it on, it does so automatically by reacting to water and pressure.

Compass

Depth gauge and timing device

Many computer consoles feature all four basic diving instruments.

Submersible pressure gauge

Exposure Suit

Keeping warm is essential when deep diving, because a loss of body heat uses energy and impairs your ability to think clearly. Also, as water pressure increases, your exposure suit compresses, thereby causing it to lose insulation at depth. An exposure suit you can wear comfortably at 60 feet (18 metres) may not be warm enough at 120 feet (36 metres). Remember, as your exposure suit compresses you will also lose buoyancy.

Due to the drop in water temperature at increased depth, you may need to add a hood, gloves, or a vest.

Exposure Suit

Cold water hastens the onset of nitrogen narcosis and decompression sickness, two potential hazards when deep diving. You may need a thicker exposure suit, or even a dry suit, due to the drop in water temperature at increased depth at some dive sites. You may also need to add a hood, gloves, or a vest.

When using a dry suit, it is the undergarment that actually provides warmth in cold water. The dry suit itself may keep you dry, but it provides no insulation from the cold. Before using a dry suit you should read the owner's manual and follow the manufacturer's guidelines. It is recommended that you take an orientation to dry suit diving or an SSI Specialty Course in Dry Suit Diving.

Special Equipment

Now that we have discussed all the basic pieces of the Total Diving System that are required on every dive (not just every deep dive), let us go on and analyze the equipment that has special applications to deep diving.

Lights

Because light and color are lost at depth, a dive light will make it easier to read gauges, to signal your buddy, or simply to restore color to the marine life. You should carry a large primary light as well as a smaller backup light that can be stored in a BC pocket or attached to a BC strap. Be sure both lights are fully charged or have fresh batteries before each dive. The light should also be equipped with a lanyard that can be secured to your wrist.

Because light and color are lost at depth, a dive light will make it easier to read gauges, to signal your buddy, or simply to restore color to the marine life.

You and your buddy may also want to attach a battery-powered light or chemical glow stick to your cylinder for emergency purposes, in case you should happen to get separated under water or on the surface. Another good habit is to mark the ascent/descent line with a strobe light so it can be easily seen from some distance away, even in poor visibility.

Dive Tables and Slate

You may want to carry your submersible, plastic SSI Dive Tables on every dive. This allows you to do contingency planning under water should your dive plan change. You should also write your dive plan on a slate that is carried with you. The slate can also be used to refigure your dive plan, record your compass setting, and for communication with your buddy. Securely attach the slate to your BC so it is easily accessible and cannot be lost, yet stays out of your way.

Diver's Tool

A diver's tool can be valuable on your dive should you become entangled in a net, rope, fishing line, kelp, or any other material. Your buddy can easily assist in freeing you if he or she has a diver's tool. If not, valuable bottom time can be wasted in attempting to become untangled, not to mention the obvious safety concerns. For greater ease in locating your tool, it is recommended that each diver carry two tools, one on the lower body and one on the upper body.

Spare Parts and Repair Kit

Because a properly maintained Total Diving System is so important to deep diving, last minute adjustments or field repairs may be necessary to prevent having to cancel a dive due to equipment problems. A complete spare parts and repair kit can come in handy for both your and your buddy's equipment, or any fellow divers in need.

Spare parts and repair kit.

The SSI Equipment Service Program

Your SSI Dive Center may offer the SSI Equipment Service Program, a complete maintenance program designed to keep the components of your Total Diving System performing to the best of their potential. Below is an explanation of each of the services that make up the SSI Equipment Service Program.

Air Delivery System Protection

Regulators are totally disassembled and cleaned in a special cleaning solution. High-pressure and low-pressure seats are replaced along with all dynamic o-rings, exhaust valves, and high pressure filters. Performance tests are conducted to manufacturer warranty specifications.

Nitrox Air Delivery System Protection

This is the same as Air Delivery System Protection, but is performed on Nitrox equipment. A green Nitrox hose sleeve is used to mark your Nitrox Air Delivery System rather than a yellow hose sleeve.

Information System Protection

Submersible pressure gauges, depth gauges, pressure activated dive timers, and dive computers are checked for accuracy in a pressure vessel, and the indicated readings versus true readings are noted.

Buoyancy Control System Protection

Buoyancy compensators are inspected for buckle strap tension and bladder seam integrity. Inflator mechanisms are disassembled, cleaned and rebuilt, the inner bladder rinsed with B.C. conditioner and over-pressure release valves are cleaned and tested for proper operation, all to manufacturer warranty specifications.

Visual Inspection Protection (and Visual Plus®)

Annually, cylinders are inspected internally and externally for rust and corrosion to the standards of DOT and CGA. It is suggested that aluminium cylinders be tested with Visual Plus to ensure the integrity and strength of the neck and threads.

Exposure System Protection

Services are available for exposure suits (wet and dry). Minor repairs are done in house and alterations are done with the original manufacturer.

When you have your equipment serviced or repaired, take along your SSI Total DiveLog so the technician can record the service. This will be valuable should you decide to upgrade your equipment someday.

Surface Support

Note: The following support equipment and personnel are recommended for deep diving. The final decision on the use of surface support should be made by the buddy team and the diving instructor if appropriate.

In addition to the equipment you need for your dive, you must also consider what surface support equipment to use. This additional equipment should be available if, by chance, some sort of accident should occur. Due to the nature of deep diving, accidents are, unfortunately, a concern, so it is prudent to be prepared.

Surface support includes not only equipment, but also personnel and an accident management plan.

Let us take a look at some of the recommended surface support you should prepare for each deep dive. Remember, the deeper you are diving, and the more hazardous the conditions, the more important surface support will be to your safety.

Support Personnel

When deep diving, one member of the dive group should always be left on the surface. This person can assist in entries and exits, radio for help, or offer aid to divers who need help on the surface. If you are diving on a charter boat or with a group, the boat captain or group leader may stay on the boat. If you are diving with

When deep diving, one member of the group should always be on the surface.

your friends, one of the group should take turns as the support person. Either way, this person should be a competent individual who knows how to use the emergency equipment and communications system, and if boat diving, how to operate the boat and anchor.

Descent/Ascent Line

A stable ascent/descent line is a valuable diving tool, especially when diving off a boat or in limited visibility. When diving, a line helps you make a more controlled ascent and descent. This line can either be the anchor line of the boat, or a weighted drop line that is either attached to the boat, or a float on the surface that is weighted or attached to the bottom.

When deep diving, it is a good idea to have an extra cylinder with two second-stages tied off at 15 feet (5 metres).

Safety Stop Cylinder and Line

When deep diving, it is a good idea to have an extra cylinder with two second stages tied off at 15 feet (5 metres) to a separate safety line, or to the ascent line. Before the dive, be sure to check the pressure in the cylinder, and then turn the air off before tying it off under water.

Do not count on using the tied off cylinder as part of your dive plan, it is there for emergency use should you run low on air during your safety stop. Proper planning and execution should prevent this situation.

Transportation

If deep diving from a boat, be sure to have rapid transportation to shore in case of an emergency, and the ability to radio for help.

DIVER DIAMOND
KNOWLEDGE · SKILLS · EQUIPMENT · EXPERIENCE
SS/ SCUBA SCHOOLS INTERNATIONAL

When boat diving, tie the ascent/descent line off midship and tie the extra cylinder to it. The line should be weighted so it hangs straight down. You may want to put some extra weights on the line in case you or your buddy are too positively buoyant at the end of the dive. Do not use an anchor line or a line tied off the back of the boat, because the wave action will not allow you to hang at a constant depth of 15 feet (5 metres).

When diving from shore, you can use some type of surface flotation that the descent line can be tied to. The descent line float should be able to support the weight of all the divers while they are making the 15 foot (5 metre) safety stop.

Surface Marker

A surface marker that the underwater team can use to signal the support personnel on the surface, if assistance is needed under water, should also be set. A surface marker can simply be a float with a line and weight attached to it. Attached to this line should be a slate and pencil that the divers can use to write a message on. By tugging on the line, the support people can see the float on the surface move and know to pull up the line and get the message off the slate. This can come in handy if extra cylinders or weights are needed for the safety stop, or if some other sort of emergency has taken place.

Deep divers can utilize the surface marker to signal the support personnel when they need help.

Oxygen

Regardless of where you deep dive, be sure to have an adequate supply of 100% oxygen easily accessible in case of a diving emergency. It has been proven that 100% oxygen is effective first aid for diving accidents. More information on the use of oxygen is available from the SSI Diver Stress and Rescue program.

First Aid Kit

A professional-grade First Aid kit with all the required contents should also be available at the dive site, or on the boat. A good First Aid manual is also a necessity. It is recommended that all divers receive first aid and CPR training. Your local SSI Dive Center may offer training in first aid and CPR, which is recognized by SSI as a non-diving specialty.

Radio/Communications

If you are boat diving, a radio should be available to call for transport or assistance in case of an emergency. If you are shore diving, a telephone should be nearby, or a portable telephone or radio should be taken with you to the site.

Accident Management Plan

An accident management plan not only includes having the necessary equipment available, but it also includes having the proper training and access to emergency medical personnel. Your plan should include the phone/radio numbers of the nearest emergency medical service (EMS). It is also a good idea to let your buddy know about your past medical history which may be of interest to medical personnel, such as previous decompression sickness, blood sugar disorders, recent surgery and drug allergies. All this information should be kept accessible. You might want to affix it to the inside of your log book and let your buddy know about it.

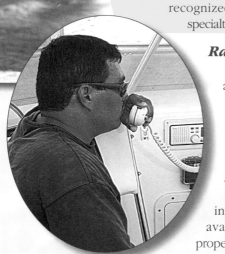

When boat diving, a portable telephone or radio should be taken with you to the site.

The Diving Accident Management Flow Chart will help you take the necessary steps in the event of an emergency.

Summary

Deep diving requires proper training, proper equipment, and proper dive execution. Using the best equipment in the world will not make deep diving safer unless you know how to use it properly. The best training in the world will not suffice unless you use proper equipment and execute the dive plan properly.

When you participate in advanced diving activities, the equipment you use should be of the highest quality available and exceed all performance requirements of the dive objective. Remember, good surface support equipment is essential for deep diving activities.

KNOWLEDGE SKILLS

DIVER DIAMOND

SSI
SCUBA SCHOOLS
INTERNATIONAL

EQUIPMENT EXPERIENCE

Section 1 Review Questions

1. Deep diving requires a top-quality, high-performance __A-D-S__ that will perform well at any depth.

2. A __balanced__ first-stage is designed to maintain excellent breathing performance all the way down to very low cylinder pressure.

3. The most accurate analog gauges at depth are the oil-filled, the gas-filled, and the __bourdon tube__.

4. Equipment manufacturers claim that __digital__ gauges are more accurate than analog gauges and the only maintenance they require is new batteries.

5. The benefit of a diving computer is that it increases your __bottom time__ by giving you __credit__ for all the time you spend at shallower depths.

6. When deep diving, one member of the dive group should always be left on the __surface__ This person can assist in entries and exits, radio for help, or offer aid to divers who need help on the surface.

7. When deep diving, it is a good idea to have an extra cylinder with two second-stages tied off at __15 feet__ to a separate __safety line__ or to the ascent line.

8. An accident management plan includes having the necessary equipment available, but it also includes having the proper __training__ and access to emergency __medical personnel__.

Planning Your Deep Dive

Often the question is asked: "Why dive deep?" Deep diving opens the door to many new and exciting dive sites. These sites include deeper wrecks, reefs, wall dives, and more. People participate in deep diving for various reasons. However, most divers are interested in enhancing and improving their skill and confidence level while taking the deep diver course. Curiosity is ever present in humans. Most divers feel the need to explore and wonder what lies "beyond"—even if we do not have the desire to look for ourselves. How many of us, while wall diving at 60 feet (18 metres) have not wondered what spectacular sites and hidden beauty lie below? Probably no one.

Deep Diving training does more for Open Water Divers than satisfy curiosity. Those who have graduated from a deep diving course have found that their diving skills have greatly improved, especially their buoyancy control and breathing rate. They have also reported that their mental awareness of depth, direction, environment, remaining air and the buddy system have improved.

In this section, you will learn how to plan and execute a deep dive with a higher degree of comfort, by obtaining a better understanding of the factors involved in deep diving.

Deep diving opens the door to many new and exciting dive sites.

Section 2 Objectives
After completing this section you will

♦ Understand Deep Diving limits,

♦ Be able to list how Deep Diving differs from other types of specialty diving,

♦ Understand the importance of planning to the Deep Diving process.

Deep Diving Limits

When we talk about deep diving, we must realize that depth is a relative term. What may be shallow in some diving conditions, may be deep under other conditions, such as cold, murky or fast moving waters. In the clear, warm waters of the Florida springs, as well as the Caribbean and South Pacific, a diver will be much more comfortable deep diving than in the colder, darker waters found on the northern coastlines of the Atlantic and Pacific oceans.

Your deep diving limits are based not only on the environment, but also on your personal experience level, comfort level, and skill level.

What may be a deep dive to you may be shallow to another diver, which is fine, for as in all types of diving, each diver must set his or her own personal diving limits.

The recreational diving industry has established deep diving limits that they recommend recreational divers adhere to. These limits are not arbitrary, but are based on Doppler ultrasound research, and have been established for the safety of the diving community.

0-60 Feet (0-18 Metres)

When you began diving in your Open Water Diver class, you began in the shallow end of the pool, and may have eventually progressed to water as deep as 60 feet (18 metres). At this point in your diving career, you were still not sure about your equipment, controlling your buoyancy, and the other new skills you had learned in your course.

The entry-level training limit is set at 60 feet (18 metres) for a good reason, because anything over that is considered "deep diving."

As you began to log dives, however, you started to feel more comfortable with your skills and started to think that it might be nice to explore beyond the 60 foot depth limit.

60-100 Feet (18-30 Metres)

You learned in your entry-level course that after Open Water Diver certification the recommended limit for recreational diving is 100 feet (30 metres), due to the increased effects of the partial pressure of nitrogen on the human body at depth. This causes effects, such as nitrogen narcosis and decompression sickness, which will be discussed in further detail in Section 4. The safety considerations for deep diving go beyond the effects of nitrogen, for deep diving is an activity that requires physical and mental preparedness.

Entry-Level
Training
Limits
0–60'

Recreational
Diving Limits
60–100'

Recreational
Deep Diving
Limits
100–130'

Established recreational deep diving limits

When divers put 100 feet of water between themselves and the surface, they must have the physical and mental skill level required for the situation, as well as more sophisticated diving equipment.

This skill level is usually acquired by logging dives under the supervision of a dive leader or with a properly trained and more experienced dive buddy.

100-130 Feet (30-39 Metres)

When a diver ventures below the 100 foot recreational limit, he begins a whole new level of diving. The effects of pressure multiply when using air at these depths, increasing the risk. Bottom time is drastically reduced, requiring careful planning and monitoring. There is less room for error at these greater depths, and only qualified divers truly understand the extra preparation and skill that is required to dive to the 130 foot (39 metre) limit.

The 100 to 130 foot depth limits are recommended only for those divers that are experienced, qualified and in excellent physical condition.

KNOWLEDGE
SKILLS
DIVER
DIAMOND
SSI
EQUIPMENT
EXPERIENCE

As mentioned earlier, the maximum limit of 130 feet (39 metres) is not an arbitrary number; it was derived through Doppler ultrasound research. By looking at the Doppler limits on the U.S. Navy tables, you can see that you can stay at 130 feet (39 metres) for 5 minutes, but beyond that, you have exceeded the Doppler limits and are subjecting yourself to increased risk for decompression sickness.

Because the U.S. Navy tables were developed for Navy divers, and not for the average recreational diver of today, the Doppler limits were established to help increase the safety factor. Doppler research will be discussed later in Section 4 under Decompression Sickness.

Note: there is no guarantee that staying within these limits will insure safety. Every diver is different, and individual nitrogen absorption rates will vary to some degree. Responsible divers plan their dives thoroughly, and part of this planning is using the Doppler limits and staying conservatively within them. Monitoring your ascent rate, and the inclusion of a 3 to 5 minute stop at 15 feet (5 metres) adds a margin of safety.

Now that we have introduced the deep diving limits and why it is important to dive within them, let us go on and look at the importance of planning your deep dive.

Deep Dive Planning

Dive planning is an important part of any dive, but it becomes even more essential when diving deep. Up to this point in your diving career, you may, or may not have been using strict dive planning. If you tend to dive shallow, or with a leader or more experienced diver, you may have either skipped the planning stage or left it up to your buddy. When deep diving, each person is an important part of the plan, and should participate in the planning process. The process provides each team member a chance to make sure the dive will fit

When deep diving, each person is an important part of the plan and should participate in the planning process.

their own objective, skill and comfort level. This way, you will not be getting involved with a dive beyond your comfort zone.

A well planned dive is safer, and besides, the planning process is a fun, social exchange, which is one of the most enjoyable aspects of diving.

Objective

Each team member should understand and agree with the objective of the planned dive. The objective may be to explore a deep reef, or to try to locate a wreck or anything of interest. If a buddy is not qualified for or interested in that objective, now is the time to make a new buddy team or change the objective.

Surface Consumption Rate & Minimum P.S.I.

The next step in deep diving planning is to figure your air consumption so you will know how much air you will use at a given depth. Your air consumption rate is affected by many factors that vary depending on your equipment, the conditions, and your comfort level. Some of the factors that affect your air consumption are listed here.

Factors in Air Consumption

- Physical size of diver
- Experience level of diver
- Stress level of diver
- Breathing habits of diver
- Work load performed on the dive
- Temperature of water
- Depth of the dive
- Breathing resistance from regulator
- Size of the cylinder
- Air loss due to leaks in cylinder valve, gauges or regulator
- Air required to equalize and maintain buoyancy with inflator

Now that we have looked at what factors affect air consumption, the next step is to use a formula to figure what your actual rate is. We refer to this air consumption formula as surface consumption rate (SCR). By knowing what your breathing rate is at the surface, you can calculate how long your cylinder of air will last at a certain depth. If you maintain a record of the air consumption rate for your dives, you can measure your comfort level, because the more comfortable you are, the less air you use.

Since the pressure gauge measures air pressure in pounds per square inch, PSI, you must know in advance how many psi per minute you will consume. Following is a simple formula you can use to determine your SCR.

Caution: Your SCR will change with cylinder size, so you will need to make a separate run with each different size cylinder you will use. The metric air consumption formula is in the appendix of this manual.

SCR Formula:

$$\frac{(PSI \div bottom\ time) \times 33\ feet^*}{Depth + 33\ feet^*} = \text{PSI consumed per minute at surface, or at 1 atmosphere}$$

Use the Formula Below for Metric Calculations

SCR Formula: Amount of air consumed in litres per minutes. The amount is figured by dividing SM into the number of litres used.

$$\frac{1339\ litres\ (air\ used)}{100\ minutes\ (SM)} = \text{SCR of 13.4 litres per minute}$$

For the purposes of this formula, we will assume the following definitions:

PSI = Air consumed in a timed swim at a constant depth

Time = Duration of the timed swim in minutes

Depth = Depth of the timed swim in feet

Example: A diver dives in salt water to 10 feet for 10 minutes and uses 300 PSI.

$$\frac{(300 \div 10) \times (33)}{10 + 33} = \textbf{23}\ \text{PSI per minute at the surface (SCR)}$$

Because the SCR expresses consumption at the surface, it must be converted to a rate consumed at depth to make it useful in dive planning. To demonstrate how much quicker your air is consumed at depth, let us use the SCR from the above example and show you what a diver at various depths (atmospheres) would consume:

Example — Consumption Rates at Various Depths (Atmospheres):			
ATM	Depth	SCR	PSI/Min Consumed
2	33	23	46
3	66	23	69
4	99	23	92

At 33 feet, a diver consumes air twice as fast as on the surface.
At 66 feet, a diver consumes air three times as fast.
At 99 feet, a diver consumes air four times as fast.

From the above example, a diver with a surface consumption rate (SCR) of 23 PSI per minute dives to 3 atmospheres, which increases the diver's consumption rate to 69 PSI per minute. The formula below shows how much time the diver would have at 66 feet with a 3000 PSI cylinder. Because divers should surface with a minimum of 500 PSI in their cylinder, you should subtract that 500 pounds now and start your calculations with 2500 PSI.

Example:
- Diver with an SCR of 23 PSI/minute
- Dives to 3 atmospheres, increasing the SCR to 69 PSI/minute
- Diver has a 3000 PSI cylinder (only count 2500 PSI)
- How much time does the diver have at 66 feet?

(2500 PSI) ÷ (69 PSI/minute) = **36** minutes at 66 feet

Should you want to calculate your air consumption for an exact depth such as 110 feet, and you know your SCR is 23, simply divide your SCR by 1 atmosphere to determine your consumption rate per foot. By multiplying your depth (110 feet) by your consumption per foot (.7 PSI), then adding your SCR (23 PSI), you arrive at your consumption rate for an exact depth. See the following formula for a better explanation.

Example:
Step 1: 23 PSI (your SCR) ÷ 33 feet = .7 PSI (consumption/ft.)
Step 2: .7 PSI x 110 feet = 77 PSI +23 PSI (SCR) =
100 PSI/minute at 100 feet

NOTE: The metric air consumption calculations are in the appendix of this manual.

When planning a deep dive, you should buddy up with a diver who has an SCR similar to yours and who is using the same volume cylinder. If you do not know your SCR, your SSI Instructor can help you calculate it.

The SSI Calcuslate

The SSI Calcuslate was designed to help you simplify the SCR problems and dive planning. Talk to your SSI Dive Center or Instructor about the SSI Calcuslate and how it works.

Running out of air at depth is extremely dangerous and completely avoidable. An out-of-air situation can result if divers do not realize that their air is used up more quickly at increased depths, or if they fail to keep a constant check of both their own and their buddy's pressure gauge.

Computers

Many dive computers on the market today will automatically calculate your consumption rates at depth and tell you how much time you have left based on your air supply.

Plan your deep dive so have a minimum of 500 PSI (35 bars) left in your cylinder at the end of the dive.

Maximum Depth and Bottom Time

The next step in deep dive planning is to determine a maximum depth and bottom time for the dive. The deeper you dive the less time (leeway) you have in planning. Therefore, it leaves

When planning a deep dive, you should buddy up with a diver who has an SCR similar to yours and who is using the same volume cylinder.

no room for chance. For example, if your planned depth is 120 feet (36 metres), you have a no-decompression bottom time limit of 10 minutes. If after 5 minutes you accidentally drop down to 130 feet (39 metres), you have already maximized your bottom time and will need to ascend.

To refresh your memory, the definition of depth is the deepest point you reached during your dive, even if it was only momentarily. When we speak of bottom time, we are referring to the elapsed time, starting from when you begin your descent, until the time you begin a direct ascent to the surface.

If you do not have a diving computer, you should always take the SSI Dive Tables or SSI Calcuslate with you under water so you have a contingency or can replan your dive if needed. However, since this may be impractical at times, it is best to pre-plan your dive for more flexibility by creating contingency plans to various depths. For example, you may want to dive between 90 and 120 feet (27-36 metres) depending on what you see under water. You can prepare your contingency plans on a slate by writing both the no-decompression bottom time limit and your air consumption limit for each depth. This is because your air consumption may be more limiting than your bottom time, and you will not want to stay down longer than your air supply will last.

Your 500 PSI (35 bars) reserve should be subtracted out of your air consumption limit so it will be there for emergencies.

Example: (Calculations based on an SCR of 23):

Maximum Depth	Doppler Limit	Air Limit
90 feet (25 metres)	25 minutes	28 minutes
100 feet (30 metres)	20 minutes	27 minutes
110 feet (33 metres)	15 minutes	25 minutes
120 feet (36 metres)	10 minutes	24 minutes

Remember, you will need to refigure this contingency plan for each repetitive dive because your bottom time limits will change throughout the diving day.

When planning a deep dive, be sure to limit the depth to the maximum that you and your buddy have been trained for. For example, a buddy team is planning a dive to 100 feet (30 metres); however, one of the buddies has never logged a dive over 60 feet (18 metres). The dive plan should be changed to a shallower depth. It should always be remembered that diving is a fun and social activity. This means that everyone should enjoy the dive and be comfortable. Part of planning is selecting parameters that meet the objective of the dive, but also meeting the comfort level of each member of the buddy team.

Environmental Conditions

The environmental conditions must be taken into consideration during the planning stages of any dive. These conditions may require changing the depth, bottom time or maybe even canceling the dive. Environmental conditions of concern would be: currents, visibility, surf and temperature.

Equipment

As discussed in the previous section, deep diving requires a high quality and well-maintained Total Diving System.

Communication

Communication between buddies is an important part of deep diving. You should be able to communicate any problems to your buddy, and he or she should be able to do the same. Hand signals should be gone over and agreed upon because many divers are taught or have picked up on different signals. So do not assume your buddy will understand your signals.

Ears not clearing

Important Hand Signals to Agree on, to Understand, and to Use are:

❏ OK ❏ Get Neutral ❏ Tired
❏ Level Off ❏ Look ❏ Dizzy
❏ Problem ❏ Watch Me ❏ Show psi
❏ Up ❏ Down ❏ Stop
❏ Danger ❏ Ears not clearing ❏ Hurry

Watch me.

Communication between buddies is an important part of deep diving.

After diving with the same buddies for a while, you will most likely add or subtract hand signals. However, do not make underwater communications too hard to follow. The use of a slate, or underwater communication devices are other ways to communicate.

Altitude and Diving

Because the dive tables were designed for use at sea level, when a diver flies in an aircraft or drives to altitude after diving, or actually dives at altitude, there is increased risk of decompression sickness. When planning a dive, you must understand the effects of altitude and take your travel plans into consideration.

Flying and Diving

When planning a deep dive, be sure to allow plenty of surface interval time before you plan on flying, especially after diving deep.

Driving in a car at high altitude also increases the risk of decompression sickness after deep diving.

Be sure to allow plenty of surface interval time before you plan on flying, especially after deep diving.

SSI recommends that divers follow the DAN (Divers Alert Network) guidelines for going to altitude after diving. The guidelines listed below were established at a 1989 Undersea and Hyperbaric Medicine Society Workshop on flying after diving.

♦ A minimum surface interval of 18 hours is required in order to be reasonably assured a diver will remain symptom free upon ascent to altitude in a commercial jet airliner (altitude up to 8000 feet or 2438 metres).

♦ Divers who plan to make daily, multiple dives for several days or make dives that require decompression stops should take special precautions and wait for an extended surface interval beyond 18 hours before flight. The greater the duration before flight the less likely is decompression sickness to occur.

♦ There can never be a flying after diving rule that is guaranteed to prevent decompression sickness completely. Rather, there can be a guideline that represents the best estimate for a conservative, safe surface interval for the vast majority of divers. There will always be an occasional diver whose physiological makeup or special diving circumstances will result in the bends.

♦ Further research is recommended to provide significant data upon which to provide more specific guidelines for the future.

High Altitude Diving

High altitude diving requires using a special set of dive tables and/or a diving computer that takes into consideration the pressure at higher altitude, because the U.S. Navy tables were designed for diving at sea level. You should be aware that the models used to develop these tables are theoretical, and the no-decompression limits vary from table to table. If you are planning to do any high altitude diving, you should first contact a professional SSI dive store that offers training in altitude diving.

High altitude diving requires using a special set of diving tables that take into consideration the pressure at higher altitude.

As you can see by the amount of information covered in this Section, deep dive planning is very important and extensive. During your deep diving experiences, you may come up with planning procedures other than those listed in this manual that are helpful and add to your diving pleasure and safety.

Altitude

The best approach to diving at altitude is to dive conservatively. The higher you go, the more conservative you should be.

DIVER DIAMOND
SSI SCUBA SCHOOLS INTERNATIONAL
KNOWLEDGE · SKILLS · EXPERIENCE · EQUIPMENT

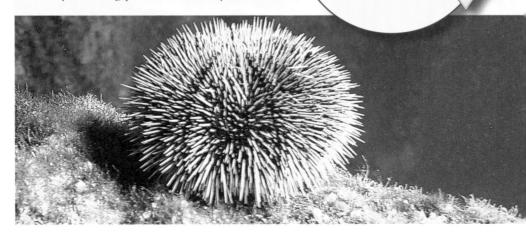

Section 2 Review Questions

1. Those who have graduated from a deep diving course have found their diving skills have greatly improved, especially their __buoyancy__ control and __breathing__ rate.

2. Your deep diving limits are based not only on the environment, but also on your personal __experience__ level, __comfort__ level, and __skill__ level.

3. The 100 to 130 foot (30-39 metre) depth limits are recommended only for those divers who are __qualified__ and __fit__.

4. The maximum limit of 130 feet (39 metres) is not an arbitrary number; it was derived through __Doppler Ultrasound__ research.

5. By knowing what your breathing rate is at the surface, you can calculate how long your cylinder of air will last at a __certain depth__.

6. When planning a deep dive, you should buddy up with a diver who has an __SCR__ *Surface Consumption Rate* similar to yours and who is using the same volume cylinder.

7. When we speak of __bottom time__, we are referring to the elapsed time, starting from when you begin your descent, until the time you begin a direct ascent to the surface.

8. A minimum surface interval of __18 hours__ is required in order to be reasonably assured a diver will remain symptom free upon ascent to altitude in a commercial jet airliner (altitude up to 8000 feet/2438 metres).

9. High altitude diving requires using a special set of __dive tables__ and/or a diving computer that takes into consideration the pressure at higher altitude.

Your Deep Dive

3

Now that we have had a chance to look at pre-dive planning and the equipment you will need for deep diving, let us look at actually planning and executing a deep dive. The basic skills vary little from your SSI Open Water Diver course, however, they need to be executed more precisely. Buoyancy control, ascents, and descents should be executed with the utmost control and precision. Plus, you need to be studiously observant of your time, depth, direction and air consumption, as well as your own physical state and that of all team members.

Section 3 Objectives
After completing this section you will

♦ Be able to list the steps needed to properly plan a deep dive,

♦ Be able to list the steps for properly executing a deep dive.

3

Pre-Entry Procedures

The deep diving process begins before the diver ever enters the water. Deep diving is all about planning, and then rechecking everything to minimize the chance of something going wrong. As we mentioned in the first two sections, making a dive plan and preparing your equipment are critical to the deep diving process. Plan your dive; dive your plan!

The preparation does not end here, however. In fact, it does not stop until the diver is safely under the water, and the dive is under way. Let us quickly look at the pre-entry procedures for deep diving.

Deep diving is all about planning, and then rechecking everything to minimize the chance of something going wrong.

Planning No-Decompression Dives

The first step in the diving process is always to make a dive plan. If you are using a computer to plan your dives, be sure that you follow the same maximum depth and procedures you use when planning using the SSI Dive Tables. All deep dives should be planned within the Doppler no-decompression limits.

Let us review a few basic points about dive planning. When planning your maximum depth, remember to use the exact depth listed on the dive tables or, if it is between, round it up to the next greatest number. For example, if you are planning a dive to 85 feet (25.5 metres) which is the bottom, then you would round your depth to 90 feet (27 metres).

If you are planning on making a repetitive dive, there are a few basic rules you will need to follow; always make the deepest dive first, and pre-plan both dives to ensure you will have enough bottom time left to complete your second dive. For example, if you do not take the time to plan through your second dive, you may find that you will need a surface interval of almost 6 hours in order to make two 100 foot (30 metre) dives in one day. If you do not plan ahead, you may end up making your second dive to only 40 feet (12 metres).

If you are planning on making a repetitive dive, always make the deepest dive first, and pre-plan both dives to endure you will have enough bottom time.

The planning stage is more than a time to make a dive profile; it is also a time for buddies to talk about hand signals, to learn about each others equipment and how it functions, and to discuss important topics such as a lost buddy procedure. For example, you should know how your buddy's power inflator operates and what kind of alternate air source he has in case of an emergency. The more thorough the plan, the higher the comfort level on the dive. Your SSI Total DiveLog page will step you through this process.

Do not plan a dive deeper than a buddy team member has been certified to, or feels comfortable doing.

Getting Ready

The dressing stage is important because it allows the diver to re-analyze his or her equipment and make sure it is functioning properly. It also allows you to make any last minute adjustments to equipment to make sure it fits more comfortably. This stage is also an indicator of the diver's stress level. Any discomfort will probably surface in the form of stalling, preoccupation, irritability, frustration and difficulty with equipment. Any abnormal behavior should be addressed, and any diver should be allowed to abort the dive if necessary.

More information on stress can be learned about in an SSI Diver Stress and Rescue course, available at your local SSI Dive Center.

KNOWLEDGE SKILLS **DIVER DIAMOND** *SSI* EQUIPMENT EXPERIENCE

Proper Weighting

Proper weighting and buoyancy control are two important skills for diving comfort—especially at depth. When you dive deep, the water pressure will greatly reduce the buoyancy in your exposure suit and BC as the air inside them compresses. This will make you negatively buoyant at depth. So why not just take some weight off your weight belt? The problem is, although you may be negative at depth, as you surface with lower cylinder pressure you become positively buoyant, sometimes too buoyant to make a normal ascent or to stop at 15 feet (5 metres) for a safety stop. This is very dangerous when deep diving. The key is proper weighting at the surface before you make your dive and proper buoyancy adjustment during the dive.

You may have already learned how to weight yourself in your Open Water Diver course, however, when you were only diving in shallow water for training, it was acceptable to weight yourself neutral on the surface. For deep diving, you may want to start slightly negative and take other factors into consideration such as cylinder buoyancy, because the buoyancy of a cylinder can vary drastically from when it is full to when it is low. For example, an aluminium 80 (2264 litres) may be 2 pounds (.9 kgs) negative when it is full at the surface, but be 4 pounds (1.8 kgs) positive at the end of the dive when it is almost empty. In contrast, a 71.2 cubic foot (2015 litres) steel cylinder is approximately 11 pounds (5 kgs) negative when it is full, and remains 5-6 pounds (2.2-2.7 kgs) negative when it is empty. You can see how cylinder buoyancy can dramatically affect your weighting at the beginning and end of a dive. In both examples, there is a 6 pound (2.7 kg) difference from the beginning to the end. You will need to adjust for this increased buoyancy by adding enough weight at the beginning of the dive, so you are still neutral at the end for the 15 foot (5 metre) stop.

Cylinder	Full Weight	Empty Weight
Aluminium 80 (2264 litres)	-2 lbs. (.9 kgs)	+4 lbs. (1.8 kgs)
Steel 71.2 cu. ft. (2015 litres)	-11 lbs. (5 kgs)	-5 lbs. (2.2 kgs)

Another way to perfect your weighting is to keep a precise record in your SSI Total DiveLog for each dive, whether it was in fresh or salt water, what type of exposure suit was worn, what type of cylinder was used, and how much weight you used. At the end of the dive, record whether you were neutral, negative or positive during your 15 foot safety stop. After experimenting on numerous dives, you will have a good record to begin referring to for future dives. You can record this information on the Proper Weighting Tables in your SSI DiveLog. Because a diver's body composition and comfort level affect weighting, there is no exact formula for how much weight to add for each type of cylinder. Use the buoyancy chart in the appendix as a guideline, or ask your SSI Dive Center about the buoyancy information for your cylinder.

Pre-Entry Buddy Check

Once you and your buddy are dressed, properly weighted and ready, perform a pre-entry buddy check. This check may detect potential problems such as tangled hoses, loose weight systems, dangling alternate air sources, or low cylinder pressure. Quickly recheck each others equipment and reconfirm important parts of the dive plan.

Once again, either diver should feel comfortable aborting the dive at this point if they are uncomfortable.

Surface Procedures

After you and your buddy enter the water, take a moment to become acclimated to the water and to orient yourself. Swim to the descent line if one is available, and reconfirm your compass heading if necessary. Once you are both comfortable, record the time on your slate or calcuslate, set your computer or watch, and descend, unless you are diving with a computer, which will record the information for you.

Descent Procedures

Proper descent procedures include going down feet first, with the power inflator in your left hand, while facing your buddy.

Descent procedures should be discussed during the pre-dive process if they will vary from a standard descent. For example, this may include when more than two divers are diving together, or when a line is not going to be used.

Proper descent procedures include going down feet first, with the power inflator in your left hand while facing your buddy. You must remain aware of your buddy's needs at all times, and be on the lookout for general problems. Your descent rate should not exceed your comfort level, or a maximum rate of 75 feet (22.5 metres) per minute. Experts agree that this is as fast as the average diver can descend without experiencing potential problems. Faster descents may cause squeezes, disorientation or an out-of-control situation. The diver should be able to stop at any time, and must avoid a "crash landing" on the bottom that can damage the reef or your equipment, or ruin the visibility.

Again, proper weighting is another important part of the descent procedures. You must be heavy enough to make a controlled descent, without being so heavy that you cannot compensate with your BC to slow your descent if needed. This is why a line is helpful when descending. The diver can slow down if necessary, stop to equalize ears, readjust a piece of equipment, or check on his or her buddy. You can also make a descent using a wall, kelp or the slope of the beach as visual references.

Deep Diving Procedures

Deep diving procedures do not vary dramatically from normal diving procedures, except that divers must be more aware of their own comfort level as well as their buddy's and they must also monitor their equipment more closely.

Once you and your buddy reach your planned depth, take a moment to orient yourselves and to make sure you are both "ok" before swimming off. Because of the increased pressure at depth, your sensations may change, so take time to let them adjust. For example, the air in your cylinder may taste different and your exhaust bubbles may sound different. You may also feel different due to the effects of nitrogen narcosis. These and other deep diving hazards will be discussed in the next section. The last thing you should do is to check your air pressure and your weight system. Because of the increased pressure, your suit will compress and your weight system may loosen up.

One of the major differences of diving at depth will be your ability to control your buoyancy.

Controlling Your Buoyancy

As we discussed earlier, one of the major differences of diving at depth will be your ability to control your buoyancy. Your exposure suit will compress at depth and lose some of its buoyancy. The volume of air in your BC will continue to decrease as pressure increases. Both factors will influence the need to inflate the BC at depth in order to remain neutrally buoyant.

Keep in mind that there is a delay in the time it takes for the BC to change your buoyancy at increased depth.

DIVER DIAMOND

Inflate the BC in small increments, letting the increased air take effect before you continue to inflate.

If you overinflate, you will find yourself beginning to rise and then having to immediately deflate your BC again. Continuous adjustments to your BC at depth may lead to unstable buoyancy control. A small adjustment is all that is needed. Also, remember to clear your ears early and often.

Monitoring Your Instruments

Because depth, bottom time and air supply are so important to deep diving, you should continually monitor your instruments. You should make sure that you do not stay down longer or dive any deeper than you had planned, and that you begin your ascent with enough air in your cylinder to make a safe ascent.

Failure to monitor your instruments could lead to an inadvertent decompression or a low air situation. When you dive deep, dive smart and stick to your plan.

Orientation and Navigation

It is extremely important to know where your exit point is at all times during the dive. In tropical water with near-infinite visibility, this is usually not difficult. However, current, kelp, and similar-looking reef formations can disorient you. In turbid water, you often cannot see more than a few feet, and on deep dives, surfacing to determine your location is impractical. You must be able to find your way to the ascent line so you can make your safety stop. If your air should begin to run low, it is important that you can find the ascent line.

You may want to take a compass heading for your destination before entering the water, just as a back up.

If you are comfortable using natural navigation, be sure and note any landmarks or reference points that will lead you back to the ascent line. If the visibility does not lend itself to natural navigation, or if you feel more comfortable using a compass, be sure to take a heading before you enter the water, and constantly monitor the compass to make sure you stay on course. If you are boat diving where there is a current, you may want to take your compass heading in the direction of the anchor line. This way, if you cannot find the anchor line when it is time to ascend you can swim into your compass heading (into the current), do your 15 foot (5 metre) safety stop in mid-water and still surface in front of the boat. This can help prevent drifting down current from the boat.

Navigation skills are important to all divers; if you are not familiar or not comfortable with navigation techniques, you should take a Navigation Specialty course from your SSI Dive Center.

Communicating With Your Buddy

You and your buddy should stay in constant communication when deep diving. Communication increases your comfort level and allows you to spot any problems in your buddy or relay any problems you may be having. Monitor yourself and your buddy for the effects of nitrogen narcosis which will be discussed in the next section.

Lost Buddy Procedure

Buddies should always stay within an arms reach of each other; but due to unforeseen circumstances you and your buddy may get separated under water. A lost buddy procedure should be discussed in the planning phase so each dive buddy will know what actions to take. A recommended procedure is to return to the ascent line immediately upon separation, and then wait for a reasonable amount of time before ascending for help. How long you wait will depend on your depth, your air supply, your available bottom time, and the urgency of the situation. If your buddy is in danger, you will want to get help as quickly as possible.

If your buddy is not waiting for you on the surface, you should instigate search procedures. It is not advisable for you to aid in the search if it could put you in danger of decompression sickness. You must weigh the risk/benefit of the situation before getting back into the water. The safety support personnel on the boat should make the search, or you should radio for help. These emergencies are why you arrange for support people and equipment.

It is not worth risking one life for another, especially if it is possible to get outside help.

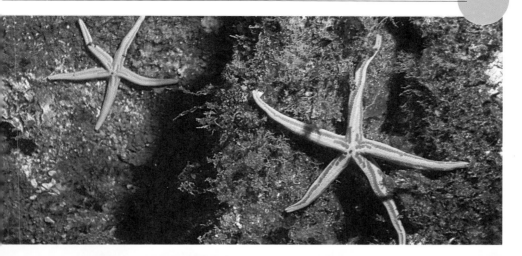

Ascent Procedures

Before it is time to ascend, return to the ascent line and your exit point. If you are diving in limited visibility or an unfamiliar area, a compass is handy to help find the ascent line. You do not want to get lost at 100 feet/30 metres when your air is running low.

The first step to a proper ascent is knowing when to ascend. When deep diving, your air supply must be constantly monitored so you have adequate air for a slow ascent and a long safety stop, while still reaching the surface with a 500 psi/35 bar reserve. There is a formula you can use to help ensure that you will have an adequate air supply for your ascent: for every 10 feet (3 metres) you must ascend, reserve 100 pounds of air (7 bars). For example, this means that if you are diving at 100 feet (30 metres), you will need to allow 1000 psi (68 bars) of air for the ascent and safety stop. When you add your 500 psi reserve to the 1000 psi, this means you must begin your ascent when you are down to 1500 psi. Because this formula is conservative, it should work for even the fastest breathers. However, it is only a guideline; you may need to adjust the formula to fit your breathing pattern.

Safety Stop

1000 PSI (68 bars)

100 feet (30 metres)

For every 10 feet (3 metres) you must ascend, reserve 100 pounds of air (7 bars).

When it is time for you and your buddy to ascend, start by quickly checking each other and your equipment to make sure all is "ok." When the team is ready to ascend, you and your buddy should face each other and start a controlled ascent at a rate of 30 feet or 9 metres per minute or less. If a line is used, hold it in one hand and your instruments in the other, you can monitor your rate of ascent and slow it down if necessary. A 30 foot (9 metre) per minute ascent rate means that you will ascend 10 feet (3 metres) every 20 seconds. Most dive computers will monitor this for you. Use caution when you get about 40 feet or 12 metres from the surface, because the air in your BC will be expanding to a volume that can make you ascend too fast.

Some divers have poor buoyancy control during descent, during the dive, and during the ascent. Buoyancy control is the single most important skill for divers to master.

You and your buddy should be within an arms length of each other during the ascent in case you need to help each other, and whenever possible, use an ascent line. You can also make an ascent using a wall, kelp, or the slope of a beach so you have both a visual reference point, and something to grab onto if you begin ascending out of control.

It will be easier to control your ascent if you gently kick to the surface, rather than floating up as your BC inflates. As mentioned earlier, the air in your BC will expand upon ascent, causing you to vent air from it rather than inflate it.

The air in your BC will expand upon ascent, causing you to vent air from it, rather than inflate it.

If you are diving from a boat, it may have a safety stop bar that hangs at 15 feet (5 metres) below the boat. A bar is nice because it allows a group of divers to make a safety stop all at once.

It can be difficult to hover at 15 feet (5 metres) without a line, even if you have excellent buoyancy control.

Current or surge can cause you to drift away from your exit point and make you kick or swim to stay in place, if you do not have anything to hold onto. An ascent line provides stability and control for deep divers. If you are diving in an area with a shallow coral reef or kelp bed, you can also end your dive by exploring this shallow area instead of making a safety stop. This can be a lot more interesting than hanging on a line, as long as you maintain a depth of approximately 15 feet (5 metres). No matter what method you choose, you should make a safety stop at 15 feet (5 metres) for 3 to 5 minutes after diving deep. The value of the 3-5 minute safety stop came out of the workshop held by the American Academy of Underwater Sciences in 1989, and at that time was shown to help lower the chances of decompression sickness.

You should make a safety stop at 15 feet (5 metres) for 3 to 5 minutes after deep diving.

3

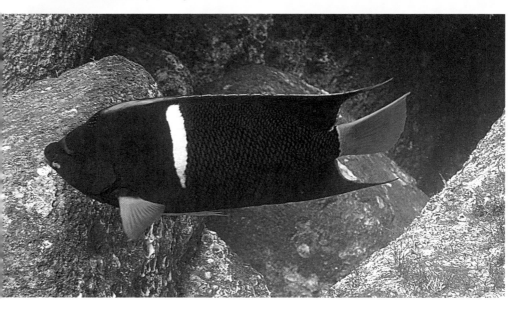

Some deep, wreck divers carry an emergency line with them which is called an "up-line." Should a diver not be able to find or return to the anchor line for the ascent, the diver can hook the up-line to the wreck and ascend from this point. When the diver reaches 15 feet (5 metres) for the safety stop, the up-line will allow them to maintain this exact depth because of the tension created between the wreck and the positively buoyant diver. SSI Dive Centers that specialize in wreck diving can assist you in how to use an up-line.

15'

Tension on up-line keeps diver at 15'

Deep diving can be a safe and exciting activity through proper planning, preparation and execution. Deep diving requires constant monitoring of your buoyancy, instruments, and your own and your buddy's physical state. As we have mentioned many times, there is less room for error when diving at depth. Deep diving also introduces certain hazards due to the increased pressure at depth. Let us move on to Section 4 and look at these Increased Hazards of Deep Diving.

Deep divers can utilize an up-line for maintaining 15 feet (5 metres) during a safety stop.

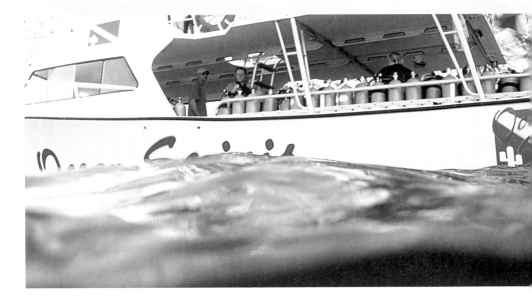

Section 3 Review Questions

1. All deep dives should be planned within the _Doppler_ _no_ - _decompression_ limits.

2. For deep diving, you will need to start slightly _negative_ and take other factors into consideration such as _Cylinder_ buoyancy, because the buoyancy of a cylinder can vary drastically from when it is full, to when it is low.

3. Your descent rate should not exceed your comfort level, or a maximum rate of _75_ _feet_ per minute.

4. Continuous adjustments to your BC at depth may lead to _Unstable_ buoyancy control.

5. If you are diving in limited visibility or in an unfamiliar area, a _Compass_ is handy to help find the ascent line.

6. There is a formula you can use to help ensure that you will have an adequate air supply for your ascent: for every 10 feet (3 metres) you must ascend, reserve _100_ _Pounds_ of air.

7. A 30 foot-per-minute (9 metres) ascent rate means that you will ascend 10 feet (3 metres) every _20_ seconds.

8. You can also make an ascent using a wall, kelp, or the slope of a beach so you have both a _visual_ _reference_ _point_, and something to grab onto if you begin ascending out of control.

Potential Hazards of Your Deep Dive

4

Because of the nature of deep diving and the effects of pressure, deep divers will always be at an increased risk for problems and accidents. This risk will be lessened through education and by understanding the potential hazards a deep diver may encounter. This increased knowledge allows a diver to plan ahead and to know what signs and symptoms to look for to avoid an accident.

Section 4 Objectives
After completing this section you will

♦ Understand the hazards of deep diving,

♦ Know how to minimize the hazards of deep diving,

♦ Be able to list the steps to manage an accident.

Potential Hazards

Not all potential hazards are life threatening or dangerous, however, they can be serious enough to require cancellation of the dive. If not dealt with immediately, they may escalate into a serious problem.

Nitrogen Narcosis

High concentrations of nitrogen under pressure have a narcotic effect on humans. It can create an abnormal sense of euphoria and well-being, nervous symptoms, and a slowing down or dulling of the normal functions of the brain. It is not known exactly why nitrogen has this effect. A diver who is "narced" may have difficulty doing things that would normally be easy, such as reading instruments, making decisions, operating a BC, or communicating with a buddy. Nitrogen

4

narcosis can cause dizziness or disorientation and if the diver continues to descend, eventual unconsciousness.

Some divers experience mild symptoms of narcosis at depths as shallow as 60 feet (18 metres), while some divers do not seem to be seriously affected at great depths. There is no time element involved in the onset of narcosis. Symptoms can occur immediately at depth, or can wait until the dive is well under way.

Most deep diving experts agree that it is possible for humans to "adapt" to the effects of nitrogen narcosis by working up to greater depths through repeated exposures. However, a diver's susceptibility may change from day to day or from dive to dive.

It is impossible to predict whether you will be affected by nitrogen narcosis, and if so, to what degree.

Should you experience any unusual feelings at depth, signal your buddy and ascend until the feelings dissipate. By ascending to a lesser depth, you lower the partial pressure of the nitrogen and the symptoms go away. After the symptoms are gone, you may want to try going back down. Quite often, the diver will not experience narcosis at the same depth the second time. However, when going back down, be sure not to violate the depth or bottom time of the planned dive. Stay close to your buddy, should you need assistance, and be prepared to ascend immediately if narcosis reoccurs.

Do not attempt to descend again if your buddy is not near you, watching you, or able to assist you.

Whenever a diver gives the "up" signal, both buddies should respond by starting up. Do not take time at the bottom to ask why; just go up. After ascending a few feet, you can stop and communicate with your buddy. Remember, any diver may abort a dive at any time. This is why it is important to dive with buddies of similar experience and ability.

Minimizing Narcosis

The effects of narcosis may be minimized by staying in good physical condition, eating a well-balanced diet, getting plenty of rest, and maintaining a regular exercise schedule.

DIVER DIAMOND
SSI
SCUBA SCHOOLS INTERNATIONAL
KNOWLEDGE · SKILLS · EQUIPMENT · EXPERIENCE

Generally there are no after-effects of nitrogen narcosis, however, some deep divers have reported that the symptoms of narcosis did not wear off immediately. This may be a post-traumatic experience.

Carbon Dioxide Excess

Carbon dioxide (CO_2) excess is generally caused by unintentionally hyperventilating through shallow, rapid breathing while scuba diving. It can also be a result of a hard-breathing air delivery system, or just diver fatigue. If CO_2 excess does occur, you should *stop, breathe, think and act* to prevent stress from occurring. Repeat this procedure over and over in your mind until it becomes a conditioned automatic response. Just relax and get control of your breathing by inhaling and exhaling deeply.

If CO_2 excess does occur, you should stop, breathe, think and act to prevent stress from occurring

The symptoms of CO_2 excess are:
- lightheadedness,
- an inability to think clearly,
- a feeling of not being able to breathe,
- and a dull headache.

A sharp headache is most likely due to the effects of cold water. More severe symptoms include a loss of consciousness and possible convulsions. Treatment for severe CO_2 excess includes getting the victim to the surface as quickly as possible.

Fatigue

Mental and physical fatigue are two of the least talked about causes of diving accidents. In deep diving, it is very important not to allow yourself or your buddy to dive, or to continue the dive, if you do not feel well — both mentally and physically. One way to minimize fatigue is to gradually work down to the greater depths with a deep diving instructor.

Other causes of fatigue when diving include:
- lack of sleep,
- illness,
- cold water,
- water movements such as currents,
- excessive drag from equipment,
- being overweighted,
- and overworking.

Hypothermia

Hypothermia is generally defined as the condition of having one's body temperature fall below normal. The term is also used to describe the overall effects of severe cold on a victim, whether it is under water or on the surface. Since the water temperature can dramatically drop at depth, especially in lakes or smaller bodies of water, hypothermia can pose a number of problems for deep divers. It is important to wear the proper exposure suit for the water temperature at the depth you will be diving.

Be sure to wear the proper exposure suit for the water temperature of the depth you will be diving.

The symptoms of hypothermia include:

♦ shivering,

♦ impaired ability to perform tasks,

♦ loss of dexterity in the hands,

♦ lack of coordination,

♦ a dulling of the senses,

♦ and a lowered ability to think clearly.

If you become chilled during the dive, it is all right to do mild exercises, like swimming while under water, to warm up. However, should you continue to be chilled, you should abort the dive and get out of the water as exercise will actually accelerate the onset of hypothermia.

KNOWLEDGE SKILLS
DIVER DIAMOND
SSI SCUBA SCHOOLS INTERNATIONAL
EQUIPMENT EXPERIENCE

Should you or your buddy become mildly hypothermic, warm yourself slowly by getting into dry clothes and into a warm environment.

Do not give a hypothermia victim anything to eat or drink unless he or she is fully conscious, and then, only administer non-caffeinated or non-alcoholic fluids.

If symptoms are severe or if the victim is unconscious, get the diver to an emergency medical facility immediately for rewarming.

Diving Maladies

4

In addition to the potential hazards already discussed, the more severe diving maladies that are a potential hazard on *every* dive, become a real danger on deep dives. This is not to say that there is a high frequency of accidents on deep dives. There is, however, an increased risk of accident. Let us look at the diving maladies that can affect deep divers, so we may learn to prevent them before they occur.

Decompression Sickness

Decompression sickness, commonly called "DCS" or "the bends," is also known as cassion's disease. When deep diving, DCS is usually caused by staying too long at depth and ascending too fast. A diver can also have a physiological problem that hinders the nitrogen desaturation. Keep in mind that all divers risk the bends, even when making no-decompression dives within the Doppler limits of the U.S. Navy tables, or when using dive computers. The risk of getting the bends is also increased with deep diving.

Researchers have found in recent years that there are certain factors that make people at increased risk of the bends. Decompression sickness research is still in its infancy stage. Each year, new information is compiled and accident statistics are collected that are used to find correlations between accident victims. Through this research, lists of factors that increase the risk of DCS have been compiled.

Decompression Sickness Risk Factors

- Age (usually over 40)
- Poor physical condition
- Obesity
- Recent surgery or illness
- Fatigue or strenuous activities during or shortly after the dive.
- Dehydration
- Use of drugs or alcohol before or immediately after a dive
- Extremes in water temperature (cold dive or hot shower afterwards
- Cramped position of arm or leg
- Pregnancy

Experts believe that divers get bent without knowing it because of their lack of knowledge of the bends and the difficulty in recognizing the symptoms.

Many of the symptoms can be attributed to something else (not getting enough sleep, sunburn, lifting diving equipment) especially when a diver has been "living it up" on vacation. According to the experts, dehydration is a proven risk factor in DCS. Alcohol directly causes dehydration by withdrawing body fluids when it is excreted in urine. The best method to avoid dehydration is to abstain from alcohol the night before a dive, during the dive day, and to drink plenty of non-alcoholic, caffeine-free fluids post dive. Remember, thirst is a sign that your body is already dehydrated. Drink fluids continuously all day even when you are not thirsty.

Decompression Sickness

Signs and Symptoms

- Tingling and itching of the skin
- Blotchy skin rash
- Local pain in arm, legs or joints
- Dizziness
- Loss of coordination
- Unusual fatigue or weakness
- Numbness or paralysis
- Shortness of breath/coughing spasms
- Collapse or unconsciousness

Symptoms usually appear between 15 minutes and 12 hours after surfacing, but in severe cases they may appear sooner.

Ninety-eight percent of all DCS symptoms usually appear in the first 24 hours.

Delayed occurrence (over 24 hours) is rare, but can occur, especially if air travel follows diving.

Delaying or failing to seek treatment is probably one of the worst things the injured diver can do. Immediate treatment is most effective in preventing residual symptoms of the bends.

To minimize the risk of decompression sickness, always adhere to the Doppler limits. Do not make decompression dives and be conservative when making multiday, multilevel, repetitive dives.

Over half of the DCS victims reported were performing repetitive or multiday dives. An industry guideline also recommends that if you are multiday diving, you only make three dives per day and you skip a day of diving in the middle of the week. This guideline allows the body to off-gas any excess nitrogen that may have accumulated during consecutive days of diving.

Air Embolism

Another diving malady that can occur when scuba diving is an overexpansion problem. If a diver fails to exhale when ascending, the air trapped in the lungs will expand, rupturing the lungs and allowing air to escape into the bloodstream and body tissue. The worst place for an air embolism to occur is in the brain. The risk of a rapid or out-of-control ascent is increased when a diver must ascend from 100 or more feet (30+ metres), especially if the diver has poor buoyancy skills or panics. The signs and symptoms of an air embolism usually appear during or immediately after surfacing and may resemble those of a stroke.

Air Embolism

Signs and Symptoms

- Dizziness
- Paralysis or weakness
- Visual blurring and distortion
- Personality change
- Loss of coordination
- Bloody froth from the mouth/nose
- Convulsions
- Chest pain
- Respiratory failure
- Unconsciousness

Pneumothorax

Pneumothorax
Signs and Symptoms

- Rapid shallow breathing
- Sharp pain in chest
- Blue skin, lips and fingernails
- Rapid heartbeat

Mediastinal Emphysema
Signs and Symptoms

- Pain in chest, usually under breastbone
- Difficulty breathing
- Faintness
- Change in voice

Subcutaneous Emphysema
Signs and Symptoms

- Difficulty in breathing & swallowing
- Change in sound of voice
- Swelling around face, neck and upper chest
- Crackling sensation when skin is touched

Pneumothorax is another lung overexpansion problem. It occurs when air escapes into the space between the lung and the chest cavity and then expands, causing a lung collapse.

Mediastinal Emphysema

Mediastinal emphysema results when air becomes trapped in the cavity between the lungs and around the heart.

Subcutaneous Emphysema

Subcutaneous emphysema has the same cause as air embolism but the results are not as serious. Air escapes into the tissues underneath the skin, usually near the neck or collar bone.

The best way to avoid an overexpansion injury is to *never hold your breath*. In other words, breathe continuously. If you are not inhaling, exhale. This is especially important on ascent.

4

Accident Management

As a certified diver, you are not qualified to provide care to an accident victim unless you have had specialized training. However, you may be the first, or only, person at the scene so you should know how to take the appropriate steps for immediate care. Ideally, you should be trained to assess the accident situation, stabilize the victim through first aid and/or oxygen administration and contact help immediately. It will be your job to relay the facts of the accident to the emergency medical personnel once they arrive.

The current medical thinking describes both overexpansion injuries, including arterial gas embolism (AGE) and decompression sickness (DCS) as decompression illness (DCI) for purposes of treatment. These injuries have such similar symptoms that they should all be treated as decompression illness until such a time as it is determined otherwise. The injured diver will need immediate medical care; therefore, getting proper medical help is your first priority.

If you are interested in learning more about accident management, you should enroll in an SSI Diver Stress and Rescue course and a First Aid and CPR course at your local SSI Dive Center. It is recommended that every diver be certified in CPR and First Aid, and it would also be advantageous to be trained in oxygen administration.

Before transport to a medical facility, or until professional medical attention is available, the victim must be stabilized:

1. Remove the injured person from danger.

2. Manage the ABC's of basic life support.

3. Provide 100% oxygen.

4. Contact the local EMS (Emergency Medical Services) immediately.

5. Call DAN at 1-919-684-8111.

6. If the injury is serious, CPR or rescue breathing with the highest possible concentration of oxygen may be necessary.

Emergency Procedures and Contacts

Before you leave for your dive destination you should prepare a list of emergency procedures and numbers on a slate, or in your log book. You should know who to contact in the region where you will be diving in case of an emergency and know the location of the nearest medical facility.

Included in your list should be the phone number of the nearest emergency medical service (EMS). The Diver's Alert Network (DAN) keeps a current list of all medical facilities on file throughout the world, so you can always contact them in an emergency.

Oxygen and Diving Accidents

One of the main responsibilities you will have as a first responder is to administer oxygen to the accident victim. Oxygen works in several ways to help the injured diver and is probably the most important aspect of treatment, other than recompression. It can produce dramatic reversals in the diver's condition, even relieving severe symptoms such as paralysis.

One of the main responsibilities you will have as a first responder is to administer oxygen to the accident victim.

Administering oxygen to a conscious, spontaneously breathing person is not difficult and is considered the standard of care. Although the benefits of 100% oxygen have been proven and it is difficult to further injure a diver with oxygen, it is recommended that the person administering oxygen be trained in the use of oxygen equipment and airway management. If your boat or dive group does not provide oxygen on site, you should know where to easily access it.

Check with your local SSI Dive Center about oxygen administration courses in your local area.

Emergency Medical Services (EMS)

The second step in the accident process is to contact emergency medical services (EMS) immediately. This may be a hospital, fire station, Coast Guard, water rescue team, or any other qualified personnel that are close to the accident site.

Cycle of Life

Hospital or Medical Facility

First Aid and CPR Responders

Emergency Dispatch

EMS

Police / Fire Department

If you choose to transport the victim yourself, it is important that you go straight to an emergency medical facility such as a hospital. Do not go directly to a hyperbaric chamber. Most chambers are not staffed with doctors who can perform a medical evaluation, and besides, the victim may not require hyperbaric treatment as much as immediate medical treatment. In addition, contrary to what a lot of divers think, you cannot just go to a chamber facility and get treatment at any time. Authorities, whether government or private, set the guidelines for admission to these

Contrary to what a lot of divers think, you cannot just go to a chamber facility and get treatment any time.

facilities, and some chambers require a doctor to authorize treatment. If you get heavily involved with deep diving after certification, you and your buddy, or local dive club, may want to visit a local chamber and learn what the protocol is for treatment. It is also interesting to learn about hyperbaric medicine and the recompression process.

If deep dives are well planned and executed, there should be little chance of accident. However, since it is better to be safe than sorry, deep divers should understand the hazards of deep diving, the signs and symptoms of the diving maladies, especially decompression sickness, and be prepared with an emergency plan.

In Section 5 we will look at Your Repetitive Deep Diving and see how to make table and computer dives within the Doppler no-decompression limits.

Section 4 Review Questions

1. __Nitrogen narcosis__ can cause dizziness or disorientation, and if the diver continues to descend, eventual unconsciousness.

2. The effects of __narcosis__ may be minimized by staying in good physical condition, eating a well-balanced diet, getting plenty of rest, and maintaining a __regular exercise__ schedule.

3. __Carbon dioxide excess__ is generally caused by unintentionally hyperventilating through shallow, rapid breathing while scuba diving.

4. When deep diving, DCS is usually caused by __staying too long__ at depth, or an improper ascent rate.

5. To minimize the risk of decompression sickness, always adhere to the __Doppler__ limits. Do not make decompression dives, and be conservative when making multiday, multilevel, __repetetive__ dives.

6. The signs and symptoms of an __air embolism__ usually appear during or immediately after surfacing and may resemble those of a stroke.

7. __Oxygen__ works in several ways to help the injured diver, and is probably the most important aspect of treatment, other than recompression.

8. The second step in the accident process is to contact __emergency medical services__ immediately.

Your
Repetitive
Deep
Diving

5

F or most divers it is just not enough to dive once and then call off the diving day, especially when you have traveled to an exotic diving resort or are diving from a live-aboard boat. Most divers like to make as many dives per day as they can. This is why diving computers have become so popular in recent years.
They not only assist in dive planning, but they also allow you to increase your bottom time by giving credit for time spent at shallower depths. While using a computer is the recommended way to dive, the dive tables, though more difficult to use, are satisfactory for planning dives. To truly understand how to plan intelligent and responsible repetitive deep dives with the tables, let us go back and review the basics of nitrogen absorption and no-decompression diving.

Section 5 Objectives
After completing this section you will

♦ Understand repetitive diving with dive tables,

♦ Understand repetitive diving with computers,

♦ Understand the difference between decompression diving and recreational diving.

Repetitive Diving with the Dive Tables

As we have already mentioned periodically throughout this manual, all deep dives should be planned within the Doppler no-decompression limits. We have also mentioned that Doppler ultrasound research indicates that all decreases in pressure cause the formation of "silent bubbles" in a diver from nitrogen coming out of solution. The U.S. Navy tables were based on the assumption that the bubbles will stay in solution as long as the partial pressure of nitrogen is not reduced by more than half. This research does not take into account the "silent bubbles," which is why the Doppler limits

5

have been added to the SSI dive tables; the Navy limits have been removed to try and encourage divers to dive only within the Doppler limits. Anytime a diver pushes these limits there is an increased risk of decompression sickness.

Let us begin by reviewing how to plan a no-decompression repetitive dive with the tables. For our example we will say that our buddy team wants to plan their first dive to 120 feet (36 metres), and their second dive to 60 feet (18 metres). Let's look at how to plan the dive to see how much bottom time is available for each dive, as well as the required surface interval. Refer to your SSI Dive Tables as needed.

Let's begin by looking at the maximum bottom time available for the first 120 foot (36 metre) dive, which is 10 minutes. If the team makes the dive for 10 minutes they will end the dive as a "D" diver. Now let's take a look at the surface interval. If they sit out somewhere between 1 hour 10 minutes and 2 hours 38 minutes, which is fairly realistic, they will end the surface interval as a "C" diver.

RG   RG   SI   RG ⇒ (for next dive this day)

D   1:15   C

safety stop ☐   60

D 120 ft.

RT ___0___
BT ___10___
TT ___10___

Computer Dive (fill out .... items)

End PSI: _____   Used: _____

SAC = _____ psi/min.   Ascent OK: ☐

Now let's look at our repetitive dive profile to see what bottom time is allowed for a second dive to 60 feet (18 metres). By looking at Table 3 you will see that the residual nitrogen time (RT) for 60 feet is 17 minutes, and the adjusted no-decompression limit is 33 minutes. Thus if they plan for a bottom time (BT) of 30 minutes and an RT of 17 minutes they will end the dive with a total bottom time (TT) of 47 minutes, which leaves them as "H" divers.

RG	RG	SI	RG ⇨ (for next dive this day)

C   H   :   H

safety stop ☐ ___ ft.

D 60 ft.

RT 17

BT 30

TT 47

Computer Dive (fill out .... items)

End PSI: _____ Used: _____

SAC = _____ psi/min. Ascent OK: ☐

You will see that a TT of 47 minutes pushes the 60 foot (18 metre) no-decompression limit of 50 minutes. This allows little room for error. To be more conservative, the dive could be planned with a longer surface interval, with a shorter bottom time or to a shallower depth.

Decompression diving is defined as "a dive that exceeds the no-decompression limits of the U.S. Navy Dive Tables, thus requiring planned decompression stops to eliminate excess nitrogen accumulated during the dive."

KNOWLEDGE SKILLS DIVER DIAMOND SSI SCUBA SCHOOLS INTERNATIONAL EQUIPMENT EXPERIENCE

Omitted Decompression

Now that we have reviewed the Doppler limits, let us take a look at what divers should do if they accidentally exceed the Doppler no-decompression limits. In Section 2, Planning Your Deep Dive, we discussed how divers should make contingency dive plans for deeper depths, and how they should take the dive table slate under water in case the dive plan is exceeded. This will allow divers to quickly replan the dive and make sure the Doppler limits have not been exceeded. But what if they have been?

Decompression diving is outside the industry standard for recreational diving. However, divers occasionally slip into an unplanned decompression situation as a result of staying too long at depth. When divers fail to stick to their no-decompression dive plan and exceed the dive table limits they need some way to get back to the surface and minimize the risk of decompression sickness. This is why we use an omitted decompression procedure.

When divers fail to stick to their no-decompression dive plan, an omitted decompression procedure should be followed.

5

Should you exceed the Doppler no-decompression time limits by less than 5 minutes on any dive, it is recommended that you ascend normally to 15 feet (5 metres) and stop for at least 10 minutes, or longer if your air supply allows. Should you exceed the Doppler no-decompression time limits by more than 5 minutes but less than 10 minutes on any dive, it is recommended that you stop at 15 feet (5 metres) for at least 20 minutes, or longer if your air supply allows.

Time Exceeded	Ascension level	Stop Time
$\leq$ 5 minutes	15 feet (5 metres)	10 minutes
$\geq$ 5 minute, $\leq$ 10 minutes	15 feet (5 metres)	20 minutes

It is also recommended that you wait 24 hours to allow for off-gassing all of the excess nitrogen in your body before making another scuba dive. It would not be wise to "guess" at what your repetitive group designation would be so you could plan another dive. You do not know how much nitrogen you have actually absorbed or released. You can only approximate it through the tables, which are based on models and average absorption rates. If you have extended your bottom time beyond the limits of the tables you are already at increased risk for DCS. Diving again would only add to that risk.

As you can see, the diver's air supply becomes the limiting factor when performing an omitted decompression stop. This is, again, why it is recommended to have an additional air supply available at 15 feet (5 metres) on deep dives.

5 Repetitive Diving with Dive Computers

Dive computers are highly recommended for all divers, especially those who intend to participate in repetitive, deep diving. Computers are designed to calculate your nitrogen absorption based on a theoretical model. They are considered by most diving experts to be more accurate for deep diving than the dive tables because they monitor your multi-level dive, giving you credit for all the time you spend at shallower depths. Most deep divers appreciate this because computers can increase your bottom time, which is a precious commodity to deep divers.

Most computer manufacturers do not recommend decompression diving with computers; however, they provide decompression stop information so your computer can assist you to the surface should you enter decompression mode. Refer to your manufacturer's directions for the special functions your computer provides.

Most computers provide decompression stop information to assist you to the surface should you enter decompression mode.

Decompression Situation

If you are using a computer and not monitoring it, you run the risk of slipping into decompression mode. Your computer should be able to provide the decompression stop information needed to get to the surface. It will indicate at what depth you should make a decompression stop and for how long. Computers will also keep track of how much nitrogen you off-gas during any surface interval. This will be the most accurate reading of what "state" your body is in. When the computer says you have completely off-gassed, you can make another dive. However, should you not follow your computer, or if you omit a decompression stop, you should still adhere to the 24-hour waiting period before making another dive.

Be aware, however, that the computer is only as smart as it has been programmed to be. Certain decompression situations could make a computer shut down, or go into "violation" mode. This means that if your dive profile is outside the programming boundaries of your computer, it will not be able to make an accurate assessment of how to assist

5

you to the surface, thus it may shut down. In this instance, you would be left to make a judgement on your ascent with no data to help you. Please read your manufacturer's directions on how to use your computer for decompression situations, and what puts it into violation mode.

A word of caution should be expressed that neither dive tables, nor computers totally eliminate the risk of DCS. No table or computer can _guarantee_ your safety because of the many unknown and extenuating factors associated with DCS; however, diving with a computer greatly increases your comfort and helps eliminate as much risk as possible.

Computer Failure

Because your computer is a digital, battery operated instrument, you should be prepared with back-up equipment and a back-up plan. Most manufacturers recommend the use of back-up instruments to help you ascend to the surface in the event of computer failure.

It is also recommended that you keep an accurate log of all of your dives during every surface interval. Thus, in theory, you would be able to complete your dive profile for that dive with your back-up instruments, then compute your group designation based on your last logged dive. However, if all of these pieces are not in place, it is recommended that you completely off-gas before making another scuba dive. Refer to the owner's manual for your particular brand of dive computer.

Computer Training

It is recommended that computer users take a Specialty Course or orientation session prior to using their computers. You will learn general computer knowledge such as decompression theory and multi-level diving, and, more importantly, the specific information about your particular brand of computer such as its functions, the recommended way to dive with it, dealing with computer failure, and decompression situations. Talk to your SSI Dive Center or Instructor to find out more about becoming a trained computer diver.

Decompression Diving

When a diver crosses the line and makes a decompression dive, a new realm of diving has been entered. The diver must fully understand the consequences and increased risk of decompression diving. This is not to say that some people do not perform decompression dives; however, this small group of divers is very experienced, with many logged dives. They also usually undergo extensive deep diving training, or learn through what could almost be considered an "apprenticeship" under the guidance of experienced deep divers. They are well planned, well equipped, well prepared and responsible — they understand and accept the consequences of what they are doing.

Decompression Diving Training

The recreational diving community does not advocate the practice of decompression diving, thus it is considered technical diving. Should you choose to participate in decompression diving it is highly recommended that you seek additional deep diving training, which is available through SSI's Technical Extended Range program (SSI TechXR).

You can contact SSI or your local SSI Dive Center to find out more about SSI TechXR Programs.

Summary

Deep diving can be an exciting and challenging adventure. Diving at greater depths opens up new wrecks, walls and other dive sites not available at shallower depths. It also provides a great sense of adventure to many divers, and satisfies our human curiosity that makes us wonder what lives in those dark waters below us.

However, responsible deep divers must also understand that they are putting themselves at increased risk to potential hazards and dive maladies such as decompression sickness. By planning properly and by using a high quality Total Diving System and the necessary safety equipment, deep divers will lessen the chance of a problem and increase the chance of a successful dive!

Deep diving, even repetitive deep diving, can be executed with minimal risk. Deep dives can be planned well within the Doppler no-decompression limits, and bottom time can safely be added by learning to use a diving computer.

Remember, *Plan your Dive, and Dive your Plan!*, and you will be headed for a exciting deep diving adventure.

Section 5 Review Questions

1. The U.S. Navy tables were based on the assumption that the bubbles will stay in solution as long as the _Partial_ _pressure_ of nitrogen is not reduced by more than _half_. This research does not take into account the " _Silent bubbles_," which is why the Doppler limits have been added to the SSI dive tables.

2. _Decompression_ diving is defined as "a dive that exceeds the no-decompression limits of the U.S. Navy Dive Tables."

3. Should you exceed the no-decompression time limits by less than 5 minutes on any dive, it is recommended that you ascend normally to 15 feet (5 metres) and stop for at least _10 minutes_

4. _dive computers_ are highly recommended for divers who intend to participate in repetitive, deep diving.

5. It is recommended that computer users take a _Specialty_ _course_ or _orientation session_ prior to using their computers.

6. The recreational diving community does not advocate the practice of decompression diving, thus it is considered _technical diving_.

5

SCUBA SCHOOLS
INTERNATIONAL

Appendix

Metric Air Consumption Calculations

WC — Water Capacity: Measure of the internal volume of the cylinder.

WP — Working Pressure: Normal filling pressure of the cylinder.

WV — Working Volume: Amount of air the cylinder holds when filled to the working pressure. (WV = WC x WP in atms)

$$\text{Air Used (litres)} \quad \frac{\text{Pressure Used} \times \text{WV}}{\text{WP}}$$

For Example (Starting Pressure) .... 22 mpa
(Finish Pressure) .... <u>10 mpa</u>
(Pressure Used) .... 12 mpa

A 2500 litre cylinder has a **WP** of 22.4 mpa and a **WV** of approximately 2500 litres.

$$\left(\frac{12\ mpa}{22.4\ mpa} \right) \ x\ 2500\ litres\ =\ 1339\ litres$$

SM — Surface Minutes: The number of minutes at a particular depth multiplied by the absolute pressure in atmospheres.

For Example: A dive to 4 atmospheres (30 metres) for 25 minutes equals 100 **SM**.

$$25\ minutes\ x\ 4\ atms\ =\ 100\ \textbf{SM}$$

SCR — Surface Consumption Rate: Amount of air consumed in litres per minutes. The amount is figured by dividing SM into the number of litres used.

$$\frac{1339\ litres\ (air\ used)}{100\ minutes\ (SM)} \ =\ \text{SCR of 13.4 litres per minute}$$

Air Required for Dive = SM x SCR

The required air must not exceed 80% of the cylinder's WC, including the air required for the ascent and safety stop. A 20% safety margin is left for contingencies or emergencies.